Rejoice

sourcebooks

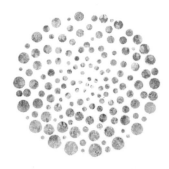

Embrace the joy of Christmas!

Within these pages you'll find warm and heartfelt quotes on what we love most about the festivities of Christmas—family, friends, and rejoicing in the beauty of winter. By threading together the ornamental letters on each page, a special Christmas message can be found. Let this book fill you with the spirit of Christmas and help you spread holiday cheer to those who need it most.

Rejoice

*with your family in
the beautiful land of life.*

—ALBERT EINSTEIN

Christmas
Bells

I heard the b**e**lls on Christmas Day

Their old, familiar carols play,

And wild and sweet

The words repeat

Of peace on Earth, good-will to men!

—HENRY WADSWORTH LONGFELLOW

Yes Virginia, there is a Santa Claus.

He exists as certainly as love and generosity and devotion exist, and you know that they abound and give to your life its highest beauty and joy. Alas! How dreary would be the world if there were no Santa Claus. It would be as dreary as if there were no Virginias. There would be no childlike faith then, no poetry, no romance to make tolerable this existence. We should have no enjoyment, except in sense and sight. The eternal light with which childhood fills the world would be extinguished.

—"YES VIRGINIA, THERE IS A SANTA CLAUS," *THE NEW YORK SUN*, 1897

It is Christmas in

the heart

that puts

Christmas

in the air.

—W. T. ELLIS

When we recall Christmas past,
we usually find that the simplest things—
not the great occasions—give off the greatest

Perhaps the best

Yuletide

decoration is being wreathed in smiles.

—UNKNOWN

It's
Christmas
Eve!

It's the one night of t he year when we all act a little nicer,

we smile a little easier, we cheer a little more.

For a couple of hours out of the w h ole year,

we are the people that we always hoped we would be.

—FRANK CROSS, *SCROOGED*

THE BEST WAY TO SPREAD

Christmas

Cheer

is singing l⬤ud
for all to hear.

—BUDDY THE ELF, *ELF*

Until one feels the spirit of Christmas,

there is no Christmas. All else is outward display—so much tinsel and decorations. For it isn't the holly, it isn't the snow. It isn't the tree nor the firelight's glow. It's the warmth that comes to the hearts of men when the Christmas spirit returns again.

—UNKNOWN

It came upon the midnight clear,

that glorious song of old.

rom angels bending near the earth,

to touch their harps of gold.

—EDMUND HAMILTON SEARS, "IT CAME UPON THE MIDNIGHT CLEAR"

E a ch Christmas I remember

The ones of long ago;

I see our mantelpiece adorned

With stockings in a row.

Each Christmas finds me drea m ing

Of days that used to be,

When we hid presents here and there,

For all the family...

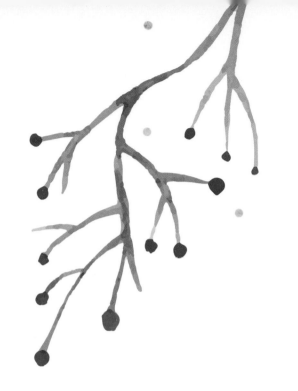

...Each Christmas I remember

The fragrance in the air,

Of roasting turkey and mince pies

And cookies everywhere.

Each Christmas finds me longing

For Christmases now past,

And I am back in childhood

As long as memories last.

—CARICE WILLIAMS

Blessed
IS THE
season

which engages the whole world

in a conspirac y of love!

—HAMILTON WRIGHT MABIE

I will honor

Christmas

*i*n my heart,

and try to keep it

all the year.

—EBENEZER SCROOGE, *A CHRISTMAS CAROL*

Christmas, MY CHILD, IS love IN ACTIO**N**.

—DALE EVANS ROGERS

*I never t hought it was such a bad little tree.
It's not bad at all, really. Maybe it just needs*

a little love.

SOMEHOW,
NOT ONLY
FOR CHRISTMAS

Some h ow not only for Christmas

But all the long year through,

The joy that you give to others

Is the joy that comes back to you.

And the mor e you spend in blessing

The poor and lonely and sad,

The more of your heart's possessing

Returns to make you glad.

—JOHN GREENLEAF WHITTIER

Let us have music for Christmas...

Sound the trumpet of joy and re **b** *irth;*

Let each of us try, with a song in our hearts,

To bring peace to men on earth.

—MILDRED L. JARRELL

Mankind is gr e at,

an immense

family

This is proved by what we feel
in our hearts **a**t *Christmas.*

—POPE JOHN XXIII

GOD *Bless* US, EVERY ONE!

—TINY TIM, *A CHRISTMAS CAROL*

Every *t*ime a

bell rings

an *angel* gets his wings.

—ZUZU,
IT'S A WONDERFUL LIFE

CANDLELIT HEART

Somewhere across the winter world tonight

You will be hearing chimes that fill the air;

Christmas extends its all-enfolding light

Across the distance...something we can share.

You will be singing, just the same as I,

These familiar songs we know so well,

And you will see these same stars in your sky

And wish upon that brightest one that fell.

I shall remember you and trim my tree,

One shining star upon the topmost bough;

I will hang wreaths of faith that all may see—

Tonight I glimpse beyond the here and now.

And all the time that we must be apart

I keep a candle in my heart.

—MARY E. LINTON

SEEING IS

Believing

*but sometimes the most rea*l *things*
in the world are the things we can't see.

—THE POLAR EXPRESS

isn't just *a* day,
it's a frame of mind...

—KRIS KRINGLE, *MIRACLE ON 34TH STREET*

When what to my wondering eyes should appear,
but a miniature sleigh, and eight tiny reindeer...

—CLEMENT C. MOORE

Christmas

waves a magic wand over this world,
and behold, everything is softer and more beautiful.

—NORMAN VINCENT PEALE

AT CHRISTMAS, PLAY AND MAKE GOOD

Cheer,

for Christmas comes but once a year.

—THOMAS TUSSER

May Christmas l end a special charm

To all you chance to do.

And may the season l i ght your way

To hopes and dreams anew.

—GARNETT ANN SCHULTZ, "MY CHRISTMAS WISH"

Christmas is forever,

*not for just one day, for loving, sharing, giving, are not to put
away like bells and lights and tinsel, in some box upon a shelf.
The good you do for others is good you do yourself.*

—NORMAN WESLEY BROOKS, "LET EVERY DAY BE CHRISTMAS"

Published by Sourcebooks, Inc.
P.O. Box 4410, Naperville, Illinois 60567-4410
(630) 961-3900
Fax: (630) 961-2168
www.sourcebooks.com

Printed and bound in China.

LEO 10 9 8 7 6 5 4 3 2 1